Explorations.

Calming The Storm

In A Young Man's Mind

By James G. Brennan

i.

Introduction.

These works were written over 30 years ago in 1990 over the period of a month when I was 24 going through a hard time mentally possibly fending off some sort of breakdown as I tended to go through periods of extreme lows where I would be quiet for days on end, these writings helped as some kind of release from a troubled mind.

I have only edited grammar and punctuation keeping the essence intact. I lost Women's Oppression Within Religion, so I rewrote that one; I also added "Obsessive you".

This is not so much a personal journey as it is an observational one looking for and finding answers concerning human behaviour.

Times have changed since 1990 when many things were not really dealt with so well. We have moved on as a society, so many issues are now more in the open, possibly leaving a body of this work outdated.

ii.

I would like to thank.

Julie Kennedy, for your patience.

Steven Kennedy, R.I.P. For the conversations.

Sharon Howell, for the encouragement and originally

putting this on paper.

Catherine McNicholas & Eli Snow,

for your enthusiasm and input.

Eli Snow for helping me with this collection

and valuable advice.

Michael Stang for lessons in "Wooden Dolls".

And to my Wife, Worakarn Brennan.

Dedicated to all who struggle with lack of confidence,

anxiety or apprehension. That's many of us.

Table of Contents

Understanding

Realisation.

It lies deep, we're unwilling,

but it's willing, mockingly so.

It comes crawling out of the hideous

darkness into the greyer area of our minds;

so we acknowledge it not.

Pushing vigorously yet so feebly,

once it's in, it never goes away

nestling in our troublesome self.

We give it time to mature

until it plays with untold strength,

a pulsating horror we flee from

creating fear within us.

The longer ignored,

the more intense its growth,

becoming a living entity

of which we have no control,

our fate may become its destiny

ripping into our inner selves taking hold

leaving us not quite sure of our stability.

Treading the careful line,

a line that appears firm

steadying our confidence,

until the violent shaking of our being,

it spreads unto the shaking of our soul.

So why not take hold from the start?

A confrontation with our fear.

Grab the root and cultivate it into

something manageable,

understand it, but never lay bare;

Underestimation.

Many dangers lay within our unconfronted thought.

Dangers that await the opportunity to escape

In a frightening form.

Adaptation.

Thoughts flirting with the imagination

within the streams of the mind, where

real fear and moral conflict hide,

in contrast, books or film

hold no such contest.

It is in the conception of the sub-conscious

mind from where we draw our fear,

revealing itself in a grotesque manner

we are afraid of, afraid of what could be;

is it possible to become what we conceive?

Slowly over time, after giving rigorous thought,

cutting through the veneer allowing thoughts

of natural process flow-through

the ever-expanding mind,

an understanding takes shape.

Manipulation of our information

gathered to understanding the minds

of others, reasons for being,

reasons for actions, a process of learning invaluable for the growth of reason.

Slowly all prejudice falls from sight,

devoid of being acknowledged again.

No disregard for point of view,

careful consideration of what lies behind

thoughts and actions helping set minds free

to release them from their confusion and inhibition.

Self-confrontation could not be attained

without our adaptation, our knowledge

of knowing what could be.

A mind completely relaxed, comfortably at peace.

Until we learn to recognise our fears,

then can we accept their horrors.

Confrontation.

Along dark alley's

roads of musk coupled with unclean feelings,

a shadowy figure seething,

resentment within festering anger,

wallowing in its discontent.

Urgent short steps growing nearer,

almost rhythmic in their dread.

Blood pumping, adrenaline flow,

confusion entwined inside disarranged thought.

The strike is made.

A sickening intoxication,

misplaced rebellious hate;

head-spinning down into

dark, never-ending tunnels of the mind.

Twisting, turning, no way out;

forced to tread the path made by

self-inhibitions until the act is complete.

The many labyrinths quickly turn

into confusion, revealing disbelief, disgust;

yet the perpetration remains uncontrolled.

The pain and pleasure stop.

No thought! Thought may stop it.

Guilt? True guilt will kill it.

The numbness folds over, overshadowing,

what little remorse was to be found.

Within our persona, the perpetrator we recognise,

nevertheless, refuse to accept.

Sanity

Fear of Failure in the Eyes of Others.

Fear of failure strong

within the apprehensive mind,

not allowed by those around

to make mistakes

within our anxious thought.

The sickening feeling deep within the gut.

With each failure sinking lower,

awaiting descent into mental demise

never to return.

Concentrating not on success

we have achieved,

instead, directing all energy

toward familiar feelings of negativity.

Allowed we are to make mistakes,

every one of us subjected

to unsuccessful deeds.

Only; those who scoff making scorn

within their mind have more significant fears

buried deep within the soul.

Doubts, if shown, would drown the ego;

an ego so very well crafted,

an ego so very carefully built.

There is no need to justify our fears;

fear is an expression from which we often shink away.

Suppression of our fear can lead us into areas of unhealthy danger.

No Safe Judgement.

An assured state of judgement,

not to touch what disgusts or horrifies

within the minds of others, respect earned

held up by pillars of strength.

The creeping feeling edges its way

into small openings of reason,

opening's left there for the ever-expansive mind.

Lethargic awareness;

the curiosity takes hold

yearning for knowledge,

compulsive urge's to learn more, discover,

compelling, drawn in by the curious magnet.

Gathering strength gathering pace feeding off each thought,

each thought becoming twofold,

until it dominates our waking conscience.

We try to push all far out of sight,

yet, only half-hearted;

curiosity is the stronger emotion.

Bouncing back, rejuvenated from absence,

thoughts and emotion run coarsely

against the grain, we tell ourselves,

"No desire to divulge".

But slowly, the invasion takes place.

Experienced guilt;

excuses flood the mind,

a new justification will see us through

fooling no one but ourselves;

ourselves the most difficult to answer to,

trickery into our false belief lasts but a little while.

So, a new state of awareness accepted,

a changing of our code,

finding reassurance and comfort in the knowledge

that someone else would be there to carry through.

Perception constantly changes within our minds.

Sometimes issues close to our hearts change through necessity.

Many times through self-indulgence.

Insanity Comes to Visit.

In our hands tightly held

never to escape;

within dwellings, in our work

money reassures.

Complacent no harm will come

an unexpected corner turned,

unfamiliar ground,

panic envelope's the mind.

No one to guide or see us through

desires not to be dragged down

the hidden valleys of fear

unseen by the naked eye;

this one you ride on your own.

Strength drained in endless reassurance

all pieces gathered together;

nothing missing so you believe,

you're never really sure.

Feelings we presumed surpassed,

backlogs of discarded emotions

come flooding back to take us down catching us unaware.

Ground unsteady, a feeling of nausea,

intensified by state of mind;

the fight is on for conscious control

it's not enough as we see our waking reality slip away

just enough for the hideous smile of ridicule

to make us realise security is not as it seems.

Where mockery once lay,

pitiful repentance now takes place.

Weary of the next haunting moments,

where will it arise? When will it materialise?

Treading the line with delicate movement,

complacency leaves the mind.

We surround ourselves with situations,

objects of familiarity to reassure us

we are coping with the world we know.

What Paranoia?

The surround to scour,

distortions, distortion not.

On full alert senses reel,

obscured the view on vision.

Understanding, confusion;

images play upon the tortured mind.

Carefully placed torture by no one, only the self.

Everyone held to accountability.

Familiar face unrecognised,

new forms are taken on,

many kinds of demons, hideous;

awful faces of self-mockery.

Unspoken whispers flow through;

imagination distorted fules torment and accusation

Try to run, the cowering corner hides

protection from contemptuous ridicule,

contemptuous ridicule never made.

Feelings built up deep inside from years of anguish

welling up, cultivated self-uncertainty,

laid there by the self; no one else to blame,

To stop; To examine? To pull through,

to prevent the pain, to realise.

To realise, yet still;

in tortures familiar, comfortable arms,

the soul of confusion is laid.

Self-pity found within paranoia,

is the sure way to self-destruction.

Time To Depart.

That stroll with death, the feeling of sinking,

of slinking off, to have no power or control.

All the things we could have been

now slipping far from sight.

"No, wait! the time for me cannot have come,

unfinished work mine to fulfil.

Good, honourable intentions never to be discovered

by those respected, admired, loved".

Reality strikes deep into the unbelieving mind,

a voice carried off into a void of silence,

never to be heard in this conscience again.

Life flashes across the background

of the ever-decreasing consciousness.

What has been and what might be,

hanging on to disbelief and hope.

The awakening slap of reality giving rise

to fear of truth about to be entered,

time here incomplete.

When can we say with confidence,

"I am ready".

In death, we find our inner strengths

our faults, our failings.

By this time, our knowledge

maybe rendered useless to this lifetime.

Fantasy

Sexual Confusion In Fantasy.

Deep inside, the feeling begins;

forcefully pushing,

strength to cause ill feelings

of intense intimidation.

The manifestation,

the expression a form to take on.

Persona delves into a world of fantasy

within graphic film, untruths told.

Confused impressions of the victim oppressed,

now beginning to enjoy

the nurtured idea of reality, unreal.

Is this how she takes on her form?

The frailty of mind misleads,

becoming unbalanced in such a viewer;

a lapse of awareness dragging them

into a reality of false perception.

The on-screen persona becomes

one who exits not,

devoid of feeling, feels no pain,

no expression, emotion was never there.

So too the victim not by choice,

adopts the persona of her on-screen rival.

His belief in her enjoyment, not in her pain;

to give her a service, experience of pleasure,

manipulation of art perverse.

Many excuses to unfold

in a mind filled with hatred and contempt.

A mind that refused to deal with

the many complexities of life,

rendering itself devoid of creativity,

devoid of expression.

Losing a sense of reality to cover-up our lack of imagination

finds an uneasy place to settle within sexual confusion.

Lost in Cinema.

An opening to a world anew,

a world filled with fantastic fantasy,

where all can go according to plan

or all can turn so terribly wrong.

A role we would rather not take on.

The hero, fears cast out, our dreams lived,

experienced for a few brief minutes.

The actor taking on our persona,

manipulating a mold,

giving a new sense of confidence

to take on situations otherwise hard to master.

To live out our pain,

we experience it through them; yet feel it not.

Attention falls to those of us who

walk away with a false sense of wellbeing;

confusion plagues the imagination, believing the role they have become.

Captivated, fixated deep within the mind;

bleeding out unconfident personality,

bearing the soul to something they know not.

Suppression of failings, confrontation cast aside,

the true self-lost in time and space.

Wandering; waiting for the opportunity to arise,

to engulf the certainty, cast off the skin,

their real own unwanted tired skin.

Assuming the persona of the on-screen actor,

disregarding our true selves leads us wide open to attacks

on personal failure from outside observers, then eventually ourselves.

Curiosity Killed The Desire.

The fantasy. A game.

Offering many forbidden delights,

delights to play with the imagination.

Exciting, enticing,

mischievous playful fantasy roleplay

With a disciplinary code.

For others, ourselves, no harm to come,

but left unchecked the time will come

when curiosity takes the lead.

The descent into a darkened place

unrecognisable to the fantasist.

Many roads within the mind,

unfamiliar, confusing, reminiscent

of the unknown maze.

The way to turn unclear,

direction falling

far from the eye of insight.

A sombre descent of confusion envelopes the fearful mind.

Afraid of concerning help,

help would mean

certain death of new insight.

A death that has not been attained as yet.

So still, there's hope,

Until caring is lost

and destiny takes its place.

"What will be, will be and is".

The need we have to see how far

our curious desires in games we play

will lead before control is lost.

Liar.

The story had begun to grow,

the larger it became,

the more intense he became.

Deeper he dug in,

Laying solid foundations

until the lie became more

tremendous than himself.

Those around him

became astounded

by the sheer refusal to recognise

how pathetic he had come across.

Surely, he knew?

He had set his face in clay so thick,

no one was to see through.

He found more than a strange enjoyment

in the lies that he told.

They had become an indispensable

part of his unshaded life,

so much so, their colours became his fix.

Even small sparkling lies that radiated,

made life so much better for those around.

Those fortunate people who could join in

such farfetched tales, and did.

He would rid himself of any idea

that an intelligent friend; one

who just might be smart enough

to figure out all was not as it seemed,

was kept far from sight.

Time left him far behind

as his lies became so many.

Keeping track became a burden,

tainting his beautiful colours

until he had realised not

the reality now surrounding him.

To lose respect of family and friends,

was to lose all purpose of his life.

he chose no boredom to keep his beautiful colours.

The refusal to believe others will see through lies

thinking one to be so clever beckons blind belligerence.

Behaviour

Primordial Temptation.

A feeling unknown, common

in all our minds.

A breaking down, regression

into basic thought.

Unrecognisable, always there.

The reasons for behaviour

we care not to recognise,

care not to acknowledge.

Refined out of society over centuries

with careful manipulation

by those who know best,

a society that has worked

relentlessly to suppress

our first basic thoughts, our behaviour.

A primordial state shows itself;

unable to harness rationality

while in vulnerable mood,

a mood of little thought

lying within the abuse of our indulgence

In alcohol, in drugs, the gambler or oppressor,

behaviour illicit,

logic and guilt pushed far from sight,

yourself to face not;

in confrontation fear lies,

fear of what you have become

or what you may give up.

The primitive state, unstructured,

thought patterns unrecognised

presenting itself in vulnerable times.

We allow our primordial states to overtake

our beliefs, our structures

in times of temptation.

Adolescence Recalled.

The behaviour we left far behind

comes crawling back

in silent sultry mood, to remind us

its leave it did not take.

Something we all share in its experience,

from which we all benefit and suffer.

Inner feelings, we find our identity,

sometimes masked but there,

what turns us on and turns us off,

the place where sexuality awaited us.

The immature mind begins

the process of adult learning,

and so to cast off feelings

to a memory outgrown,

setting aside the knowledge of its existence

a stage hardly noticed,

in period of development

needed for the sake of expansion.

We lend ourselves in times

of excitement, in times of playful mood

to behaviour unconcerned

with maturing attitudes,

wisdom cast aside;

regressing into the once held

state of consciousness

we once possessed.

Discarding all we have taught ourselves,

unconcerned with discipline,

letting childhood moods wash over.

In all of us, the child yearns to play.

We have set ourselves in pride and responsibility,

the tantrum now dangerous in games we play

for ourselves and those around us.

The behaviour we left far behind comes creeping back

in sultry mood, to remind us its leave it did not take.

Adolescence Recalled. Part Two.

Within the age of pubescence

a time of learning unfolds, with learning

comes pain and embarrassment,

recognised within times of knowledge.

To cast aside faces of mockery

used to exorcise themselves

of memories past.

Faces who have passed through this place.

To recognise it for what it is.

A time of learning, of growth.

A time of expansion,

a time of our lives which follows us

as we pass our years of adolescence.

A time which remains with us,

well into our adulthood.

The Curious Pain.

The gaze befalls the body bloodied,

nervous excitement of what is to come.

Limbs amiss, pain and horror,

Or even loss of life.

A feeling, strange disappointment,

expectations of the fate at hand.

Behaviour shameful to the concerning mind,

quickly quelling thoughts, they existed not!

An examination into lack of concern,

an understanding of natural process

for newly found emotion within the ego.

Adrenalin flow, nervous excitement,

adaptability for those involved,

living a role we've no wish to live;

adjustment to circumstance anew.

Such unfortunate chance unto ourselves?

A fear to now envelop, unease?

Relief consumes, for this time at least; the pain is not ours.

Curiosity takes its place in human nature

where death or injury are involved.

We use our discipline to hold curiosity at bay.

Each Freedom Of Choice.

Subliminal smile.

Welcoming.

Eagerness to tempt you,

forbidden delights.

Forbidden by whom;

by those afraid of desires possessed?

An array of feelings

laid out in corridors

reminiscent of the mind.

Unrecognisable world to descend;

For many, hidden from view.

Mans' dark desires,

a world experienced where

all are unashamed

to live out their wishes,

condemned by all who live in a world

where deeds carried out,

are righteous in others eyes.

No scandal perverse,

behaviour to shock ironed out to protect,

to venture not into corners

that repulse ourselves, repel others.

In other minds, they also lurk,

waiting for the revealing crack,

afraid of feelings we may possess,

a barrier to remind us not

of the power of fear

in which its grasp may hold us.

To oppress others, reminding us not

of our denying vulnerable selves.

We shun the voice of others who provoke thoughts within us

leading to fear of what we hold within our subconscious minds.

Subconscious minds we prefer not to deal with.

Bittersweet Temptation.

The temptation is strong.

We tasted it not, but there it lies,

waiting, beckoning in sultry mood,

Lavish in all its splendour.

Interested not are we,

only its forbiddance

becomes attractive to our minds,

the outer layer colourful, appealing.

We open with our bated breath;

once opened bitterness befalls our taste,

disappointment meets our expectations,

embittered surprise, yet

knowing our responding ways.

Still, time and time again we try,

one day hoping to our taste

will fall to sweet temptation.

Should that day arrive,

with all its illusions, all its allure,

will this day be the day our expectations are lowered into something we recognise not?

A realignment of perception can be made

to accommodate our cravings, our greed.

Uncomfortable Me Finds Nothing New.

Looking for satisfaction of mind, as I turn into

unfamiliar streets, something to occupy,

something new to explore, leading me

to roads anew, into a place of un-tried delights.

Examination of the surround becoming frantic,

fear of disappointment beginning to envelope

my ever-searching mind.

Strolling slowly along sleazy streets of bright neon,

looking desperately upon girls of pleasure

offering their worldly goods for hungry lust,

to take me somewhere new.

Men beating *their property* into behaviour loyal,

disgust envelope's my naive mind,

to get involved would find

a world of pain I am not ready to invite; or maybe, this is just what I need.

Sensibility returns after these few brief seconds

of unrealistic reactionary thought,

relief their experience is not mine.

I am quick to abandon these thoughts of pity;

if I delve too deeply, I shall find my peace.

So back to my dissatisfaction, as I settle once more

into its uncomfortable mood.

Offers from an empty head full of waste

to take you down that spiral staircase of demise.

Tempted; the mood is not mine.

Men of men for something new? such offers find amusement,

my feelings are not aligned.

Defeated as I trace the steps leading back towards the place

I had begun; feelings of frustration,

I found no thrill within my soul of discontent,

disappointment in the lack of my imagination,

missing creativity or effort; the empty feeling once again

finds an all too familiar home.

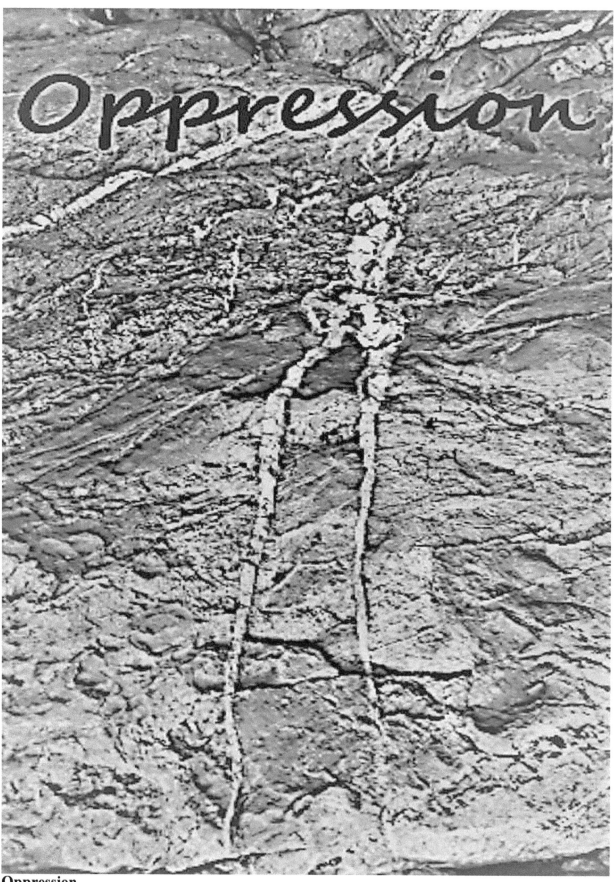

Oppression

Man's Greatest Opponent.

Looking through the window, it's a world

unrecognised by men,

a world where freedom and expression

have to be won in battle,

the right to be counted as human beings

second to none;

to be seen not as a threat,

but as a partner, an equal.

Man's carefully placed disregard

to keep women in their place

so as not to compete against his fragile pride,

pride so easily bruised, so easily broken,

too painful to mend.

An act against one man,

an act against all men!

Imposing violence to force submission,

his bidding to become her will.

His plaything, duties

he prefers to perform not, the rearing of his namesake.

Violence within sexual hatred;

to abuse the flesh

taking her soul apart,

performance against her will.

She took on his bidding,

his bidding becomes her bond.

Unworthy of respect to boost deflated egos,

pumped up with painful words of scorn,

humiliation will see his ego rise

lustful feeling's resolved

taking the inflated mind into needed

egotistical ecstasy,

masking confrontation of fear, of weakness.

The abuse of Women

sought out in the eye of the pornographer,

inflicting mental pain, not pleasure,

for many to witness or believe in.

Molding her flesh into fashioned meat

beckoning for male dominance,

feeble male assertion.

To drag her down through the ages,

a primitive mate is ideal

begging for the male provided catch,

brutal savagery to inflict upon the weaker sex

playing out in uneducated minds.

Afraid of prejudice unearthed

deep within a persona

held together by decaying morals,

confusion, frustration within acts enforced,

sinking to new depths of degradation against Women,

complications cast aside; his soul he cannot set free.

The need for man to dominate women

renders him ridiculous and inept.

Spoils Of War.

The horror unseen,

unrecognised,

no wish to be.

Rights relinquished, a spoil of war.

The priority;

the assertion of the male-dominant mind.

Lack of self-satisfaction,

the frustration of performance unachieved,

compensation: the thrill to take what is not his.

A feeling of insobriety,

head rush to gut,

egotistical yearnings,

explosions in the groin.

The right is his *for this is war,*

behaviour to be expected.

In violence, the prey is snatched,

swooping in, executing the act

with a soldier's professionalism, as he delivers his relief.

Regression into ancient memories

where morality loosely hung.

Is this what he was trained for?

To come so far, achieved so little.

His victim to receive humiliation.

as she falls mercilessly into his role play,

his aim; to reduce her into a worthless object,

to reduce her burnt-out soul to ashes.

He feels permitted this way.

Breaking her down with the insidious

face of evil spawned thousands of miles away,

graciously delivering her degradation.

His filthy body awarding her the repugnant smell of blood,

exciting him to his offensive end.

The sight of his rifle provides Perverse stimulation,

to take into battle his memories, infantile.

Her victimisation of feelings unearthed

given the excuse to be expressed,

the games of his undeveloped mind now becomes his reality.

Vulgarity plays the leading role.

A crime to be forgotten. *Hard to verify.*

Disloyalty to the perpetrator not shown.

A friend, lifesaver,

torment upon those saved.

Greater is the pain upon her tortured soul,

her very being experienced pain to satisfy

an out of control, egotistical hunger,

a victim of demoralised acts.

The first casualty of war is the mind.

Obsessive You.

A feeling which climbs deep from within,

whose keepers would say

has grown from the soul.

Passion from an agonizing heart,

a burning need from their objects of desire.

The insistence, possession,

frustration, to think only

of their own demented feelings,

mistaking them for love of their victim.

Plans drawn up, over and over.

The entrapment rehearsal takes place

until near perfection is reached,

only to befall their stumbling words,

actions nervous,

attention brings panicked

behaviour of despair.

The simplest of daily routines find upset

in yearning appetite,

obsessive behaviour acquired,

reasonable behaviour put on hold,

fear of performance less than perfect

for undesirable attention,

attention on a life,

having no wish to include

the penetrating selfishness

from their oppressor rejected.

Pain of disbelief in how someone so revered

finds refusal in their affection.

A now life ambition finds itself bowing before ego's demise.

All is right and well in the mind of an obsessive partner

regardless of the pain they put themselves

and others through.

Tales For Authority.

Tales we tell of many demons many, beasts.

Gods and devils to playfully taunt

fearful visions of the unknown.

The need to thrust images of fantasy

into young imagination's

using tried and tested methods of manipulation,

stories about terror and fear.

Suggestion plagues the gullible mind;

ensuring reality's weakening grip,

sought out by the narrators.

frightening tales,

revelling in their deception

until the story takes on its form.

Intensity from the lips of deception

coercing shapes from within the shadows,

the gullible imagination takes on a life of its own,

relinquishing control.

The deeper the rooted fear,

the tighter fantasy's grip becomes,

assertion taken to gain control

the pure mind sees far from view.

Daylight brings its saviour,

returning the mind back to the soul

allowing normality to take back its lead

in daylights waking hours.

Chilling tales lingering always in the back

of the young mind;

behaviour mindful for fear of bringing on

tales of terror's wrath.

Authority accomplished by adults

who sought out absent control.

Adult storytellers have used tales of manipulation

to control children's behaviour while not in

their company over millennia.

Civilise The Primitives.

In the forest a humble race;

tribal people close to the earth,

respect for its surround, its flow of life

respect for each other; at peace.

No overwhelming need to conquer or destroy,

to take and manipulate the lives of others;

a need for the earth,

until destroyed by men of cultures advanced.

Harmony forsaken and forgotten

in the journey to make better,

to become civilised.

Moving in on worldly lives,

convincing them of better ways

of a life from which once we came.

Corruption, ideals, the way forward.To be a man,

fight for what we're told is ours; not what we love and share together.

So with all its trickery, magic and wonder,

western society takes indigenous people,

puts them into shackles and chains

to taste a world of new delights, new temptations,

of which they are *"free"* to choose.

Western man's constant intrusion on worldly cultures

often leads to their destruction.

Ridicule You.

This desired domain, out of reach,

this domain feeds insecurity within minds of men

clawing away deeper and deeper,

tearing into their wretched lowly being,

The easier seams of confidence come apart,

the more vigorously I pull at the thread.

Tearing into the soul to take one down

into the depths of despair for all to witness.

Those I surround myself with gloat, torment,

for fear themselves becoming the victim of my derision.

The cold edge of hate to draw across my conceit,

but dare they? They dare not!

Strength of personality to assume?

For them, too hard to master.

My domain exploits its full potential,

weakness befalls my abrasive manner.

Advantage mine as one falls pitifully from sight

within one's own sorry mind.

The more demanding the competition,

the sweeter the taste upon my palate

as one yields miserably to my vulgarity.

Sweet the sounds of frailty

uttered from feeble lips.

To lead me into your domain?

Unsure you are, to mine you came,

and come you will again,

to fulfil your needs, to fulfil your yearning.

Suffer no weakness shall I, yours I shall receive.

Laid deep into your mind, scars of pain

carefully implanted, merely for protection of mine.

We pay homage to our ego's

building lavish temples

of security for them to grow.

Women's Oppression Within Religion.

In the name of all that is good and decent.

A veil, emblems, colours,

for those of second class standing.

Born into a body oppressed by men

to manipulate, feed their egos

in the name of their God.

Believing man is more significant than Woman.

God is a man! Man is made in the image of God!

Teaching and learning throughout the ages,

moulded for the advantage of men;

Women allowed by men to partake

in religious ceremony at times chosen

to suit his ego of self-important need.

To be of equal standing would mean

Women would be as important as men?

Men are appointed Spiritual leaders;

no role for a woman!

As instructed by their self-appointed,

misogynist God.

To dress women in a way to cause

no temptation for another's wandering eye,

the same wandering eye

they themselves possess.

Their God's instructions to

Keep women under control, for they are temptation;

this temptation reveals the weakness of man.

Again, all blame averted for man's perversion.

Throughout history, men have perversely

used religion to suppress the sexuality of women.

His inability to deal with his own sexuality

is responsible for his paranoia.

Wooden Dolls.

Slouching in my comfortable lazy — don't disturb my chair —

in a room full of peace and quiet

the atmosphere right for careless thought

wondering in wondering out

of lucid dream-filled plains

A magazine slips from my hand

to the floor, pages full of images

beautiful people whom most of us identify not.

Thoughts scatter as sleep holds me in its warm comfortable grip.

My dream takes me to fields of lush pasture,

leading to a small wood

sat afoot of a sunlit horizon

to finish off Nature's perfect view.

The desire to be engulfed within

the heart of this wood becomes strong;

pastoral features revealing their detail,

a precious sight appeasing my eager absorbing eyes.

Entering the darkened wood,

surprise jolts my emotions.

An abundant collage of sunlit leaves

are swirling around my spinning head;

I'm engulfed a sense of awe.

This is real beauty as here I stand, an honoured guest.

Adjusting my attention obtrusive shapes began to form.

My eyes focus on darkened figures,

twisted branches awkwardly protruding

from crippled trunks, almost as if they suffered silent pain.

My mood becomes aggrieved — perception betrayed;

in resignation I acknowledge my easily led attention to

beauty's sight enticing me away from the suffering wood.

The image brakes up; I awake from my insufferable dream

lightheaded — confused — my attention falls to the floor;

the realization dawns, projected images within pages of deceit

plague this magazine, playing on my gullible mind.

I smile an awkward smile, trickery absorbed

into the narrow perception of my naivety.

Thanks to Michael Stang.

Quite often the exterior betrays hidden torment to be found in people who the media lavishes its attention.

Sexuality

Body Beautiful.

The universal vision of sexuality

perversely moulded for dreams

of the advertiser.

The body beautiful smooth perfection

luring us into states of inadequacy

fear of our incomplete selves.

The admiration of those around us,

the tireless vocation to make ourselves

Just like them, the Gods of love,

beauty within to take second place.

Stylised sex designer meat,

no sweat no pain

no mess upon hot sheets of lust.

Flowing; beautiful,

art executed so smoothly, controlled.

Upon ourselves, our gaze befalls

attention given to imperfections.

Where is perfection, how do I attain?

No control is where beauty lies,

surprise and pleasure

letting go of fashion to perform our art,

for art it is;

not finding ourselves in awkward efforts

to avoid unwanted embarrassment.

Constant bombardment of media demands

on our physical selves

unhinges our confidence.

Unsatisfied.

Alluring faces beckoning from pages or screen

to attract interest in their delights

a world full of fantasy for the voyeur to enter;

to divulge in something new,

to have the chance to explore

release from a backlog of pent-up emotion,

feelings of inadequacy.

The excitement;

stimulation of senses

find the brain awash in lustful pleasure;

yearning for presented flesh desired,

not to receive, only to play within their fantasy.

In fantasy the image takes on infatuation.

Naked flesh of tonal beauty lusting to the eye;

to be in control enslaved to desires,

fingers caress the mind erecting wilted ego.

Strength now felt to dominate

a personality chose to spend time with;

this time will serve its purpose.

The graduation takes place;

moving toward more explicit.

Nothing left for the imagination to feed on,

where will the imagination go, how shall it grow?

To find a new movement find new games,

games to take one to the edge of reality;

reality so nearly lost.

Challenges become more distasteful;

interest obsessive, new tools in a trade,

extending excitement to genital pain;

manipulating pain for the revulsion of others

or others delight, finding they have become

victims of their own misunderstood games;

manifesting in a way that requires

no imagination no creativity within an art.

Delving deeper into sexual stress, sometimes leads us to a more

obsessive path; the urge for more growing in strength

until no longer recognised.

Perverse Kicks.

The erotic game, a need,

the feeling of something new

a yearning through generations

from neolithic man to men of culture.

The excitement, forbidden fruit,

cravings acted upon given opportunities,

compellingly addictive the ultimate sexual experience

finding pleasure from object to insect to animal

the mind knows no boundaries.

The brain awash in rebelling ecstasy

to embark on complexities of performance public,

welcoming venture's new for others to witness

while they become an unwilling party.

Complete surprise feelings of disgust

at the invitation to enacted madness.

Come and try this game it's new

give yourself over to intense hidden feelings

after all they're in us all come on over taste new delights.

Unbelieving gaze finds its repugnance.

of what could be.

The performer finds themself high on rebellion

extracted from onlookers manipulated emotion,

twisted perception fed until the next urge

finds itself in all-consuming irresistible mood.

Perversity lies in the eye of the beholder.

Animalistic Sex.

Anger,

Frustration,

exhaustive clamber for words

to tear deep into the flesh.

Scorn,

hurtful meaningful

meaningless gesturing

a need to strikeout

the tongue of a snake

to degrade

humiliate.

A moment of heat seized upon

to lose; disaster would strike.

A violent clench

writhing together

animal tendencies

rigorous hurtful

primaeval mating raw, not sensual.

Ease awash the stressful mind

a respectfully taunting look,

admirably.

Experienced, grateful of love and lust

a rebelling

yet not torn apart.

A need to take sexual gameplay into the field of humiliation,

played on equal ground to see how fused the two power players are.

Incest.

A passion of strength unrecognised by most

love flowing forbidden fruit,

excitement in knowing

within the eyes of others lies closely guarded

disbelieving shock and moral disgust.

A bond formed closely more so than

bonds created within relationships.

held in our society of ethics correct.

Not brother not sister, lovers;

entwined bodies minds and spirit's merge

alone but together in a wilderness of feelings.

Regression to primordial past

a past which knew of no binding morality.

Carefully spoken spectator scorn

disgust runs deep within the eye

never to reach the mind of reason

burning deep into the lover's being.

Hindrance not given a chance to grow,

strength built upon foundations of their scorn

laid by values carefully chosen in society's moral eye.

In a society of moral ethics

love does not run freely.

Discovery.

She was shown how to unlock her door,

the door of unlimited feeling;

feelings which had lain dormant

welcomed by her open arms,

awakened to her sensual world

a world she never knew she had;

once the student naive

who now become the master.

Taking his hand, she led him

down the path he'd built unsure,

hesitant steps he took toward

a world of dreams now pure.

Do not fear for such is love,

love is where you'll find me.

For the love she taught ever grateful

he would be.

A thousand wounds she had healed

in her love he must believe,

she's the one to set him free.

And so, he took her hand held tight

to lead him through his hindered fear,

cutting through the undergrowth

of an uncertain critical mind.

To Summarise.

As human beings, we make mistakes, some weightier than others; we punish ourselves and others when there is no need.

We all have our darker sides to our emotions, most of us push these thoughts away refusing to acknowledge them, feelings that are part of natural thought process.

We are all interested in letting out a little thread of emotional experimentation to see where it will lead us; we all know the boundaries between right and wrong within ourselves.

If these boundaries are lived within, then mistakes become futile.

Lightning Source UK Ltd.
Milton Keynes UK
UKHW030625210223
417379UK00004B/25

9 798215 058084